THE SECRET OF THE BROKEN STONE

By Barbara J. Morrison

Published by Barbara J. Morrison

Contact information
http://TheheartbeatofWords.blogspot.com
www.amazon.com/author/bjmorrison
www.theheartbeatofwords.com

When my mother was a little girl, her mother gave her a very special box. She told me that one day, I would also be given this special gift, but she would not tell me when.

My Grandmother gave the little box to her when she was ten-years-old. I am almost ten. In two days it will be my tenth birthday. It would be a perfect surprise.

It is such an old trinket box. Grandmother told me that her mother gave it to her when she was a child.

I have to wonder how many times it has been passed to another person, and how long it has been in the family.

I am especially curious as to what is inside, as I have never been allowed to know the secret.

My mother keeps this special treasure in her room by her jewelry box. I wonder if it is a piece of jewelry? Why else would she keep it there? There are always two stones on top of it.

If I could just get a small peek inside, I would be able to wait, but, I am so anxious to know the secret.

I guess I will just have to wait this out until the day that my tenth birthday arrives. Maybe I will have a delightful surprise.

It is going to be very hard to do, especially since I know where the box is kept.

I don't want to sneak into my mother's room to find out, but I am very tempted to do that very thing. I must try to be patient.

I am just going to do something else with my time that will help me wait. I think I will look at my own treasures in my own secret box.

I love to gather old stones. My grandfather was a miner of many types of stones. He loves rocks. He has passed that love down to me by showing me everything about his work and how he had to learn so many things before he could properly know what each stone was.

Grandfather said that his father, and his father before him also mined for precious and semi-precious stones in the bedrocks.

This would mean that all the way back to my Great-Great Grandfather, they mined for beautiful stones just like hunting for treasure. There are many stories about this in our family.

Look how beautiful they all are.
Grandfather has given me so many to save.
I will tell you about some of the prettiest
stones.

This will help me pass some time, and not
worry so much about my birthday. I have at
least 100 stones, but I am going to share
some of my favorite ones.

The first one I really love, is purple. Sometimes it has white colors deep inside as if it were snow. It is called AMETHYST. It is a semi-precious stone that is cold when you touch it. After you hold it in your hand for a while it begins to get warm from the heat of your own body. It is good to make beautiful rings with. Grandfather said all of the stones have a way of making a person feel good because they are so beautiful to look at, and to feel on your skin.

I am going to show you my stones with my most favorite thing:
A DIGITAL MICROSCOPE

You will be able to see how they really look close up. They keep their secrets inside.
The digital microscope will show you on a computer screen just how awesome the stone is. I love using it. I put all sorts of things under it and look closely at them.

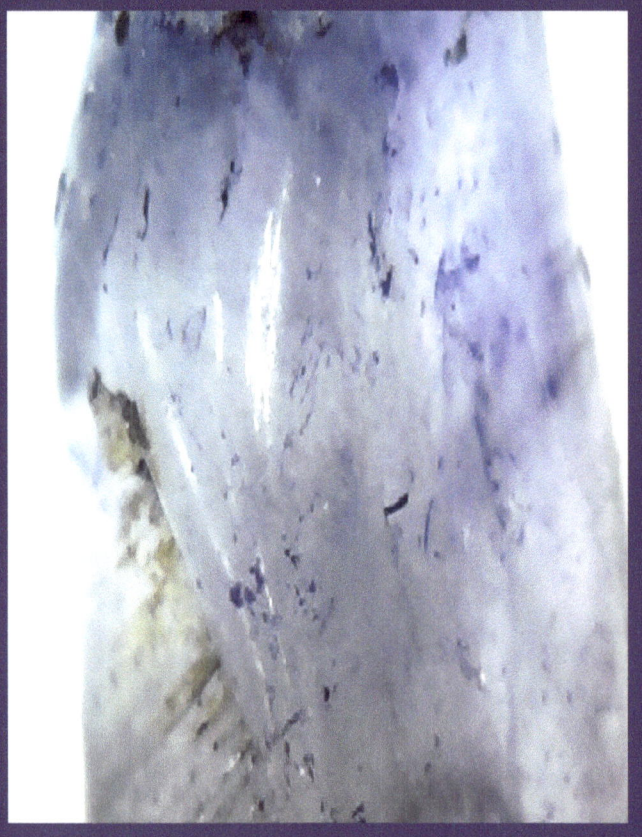

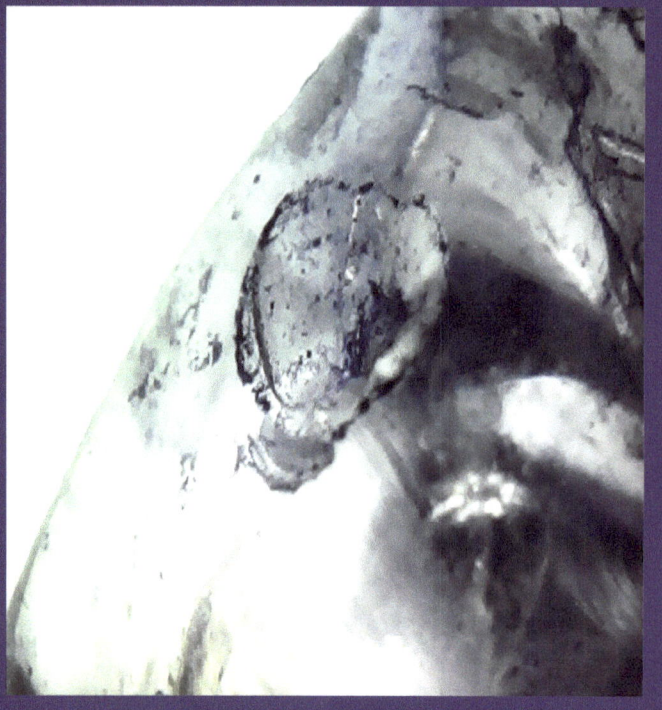

Under the microscope, Amethyst looks like purple water. Every little thing inside of the stone can be seen. There are swirls, and lines, little pockets, and what looks like snow on a mountain top, occasionally . Grandfather said that Amethyst is a stone for kings and queens. I think it is my favorite because it is purple. The microscope shows me even more beauty inside every time I move it around. I can see more and more things.

Now I will show you a CITRINE. I love this stone. It reminds me of the sunshine. Sometimes Citrine has a white snow top that looks like it has snowed on the mountains. It makes me happy inside when I hold this stone, looking through it with the sunshine. You can almost see through it. Beautiful rings are made from this stone. It is a yellow stone most of the time, but can get close to clear with hints of yellow and firelight.

Citrine has a warm glow. It reminds me of water with ice in it when I see it under the microscope. Grandfather told me it is a stone that encourages people to do their very best. It has a very clean look that reminds me of the morning sun.   I read in a book about gemstones that Citrine is the birthstone for the month of November.

This is my mother's birthstone. She has a ring with a Citrine gemstone on it. I wonder if that could be what is in the trinket box by her jewelry box? She doesn't always wear it, and I do not know where she keeps it. I am trying very hard not to think about the BOX!

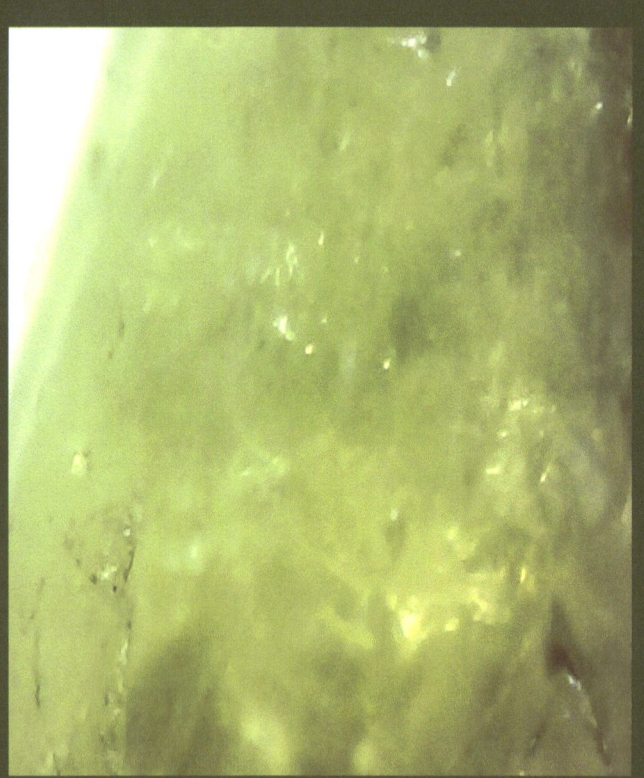 

This stone is CARNELIAN. It is orange sometimes and red at others. It can be a mix of orange with yellow light as well as reds. This stone reminds me of a piece of candy. Lets look inside and see what we can see in it.

Carnelian is beautiful. Even though it seems red, or orange, like fire, when it is seen under the microscope, it has a lot of pink tones to it.

I think the lights on my microscope make it look lighter.

This stone has a little dip in it. Inside of the dip there seems to be tiny crystals formed.

Grandfather tells me that it is like a little wound on the stone where it was attached to a bigger rock called a matrix.

When it fell away, or was dug out of the bigger rock, it caused a little break.

I couldn't see it until I put it underneath the microscope. Small little dark spots were deposited there where it was wounded.

My mother likes this stone. She says it has always made her feel happy and peaceful when she holds it. Maybe each stone has a special thing that it gives to us. Maybe all of us can feel it.

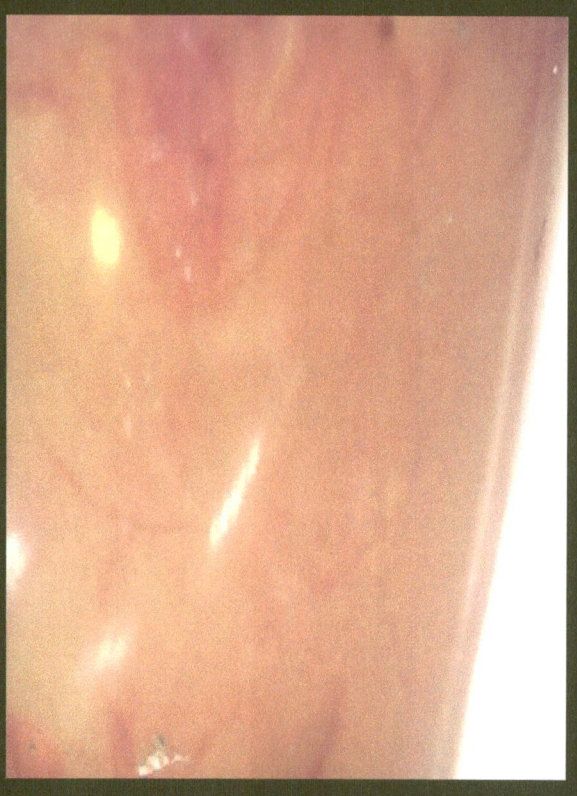

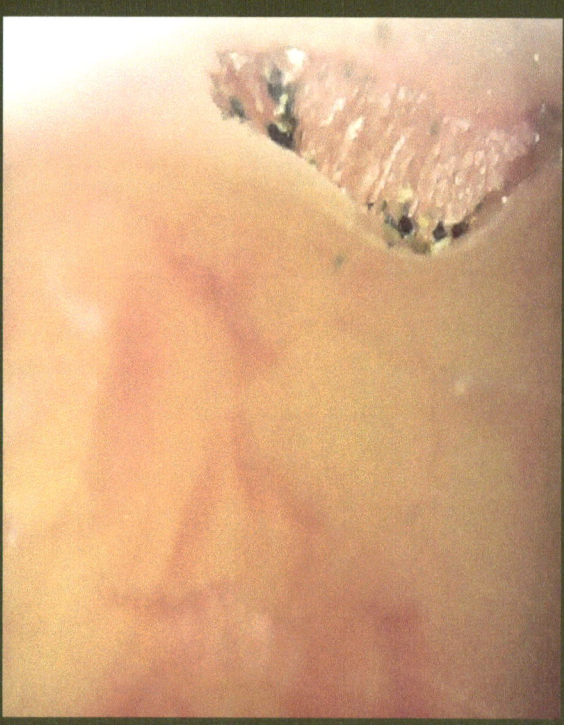

Now I want to show you a stone called Green Aventurine. It is one of my favorites too. Grandfather gave this one to me first. I love the green and white colors in it. He has a piece that was all shined up and it looked very smooth with light green, shimmery colors. It is on his belt buckle that he wears on Sundays. He gave me this larger one for my collection. I love how it shimmers.

GREEN AVENTURINE IS SO BEAUTIFUL. I LOVE OUTDOOR COLORS LIKE THE EARTH AND THE LIFE OF TREES. THIS IS A FAVORITE OF MINE.

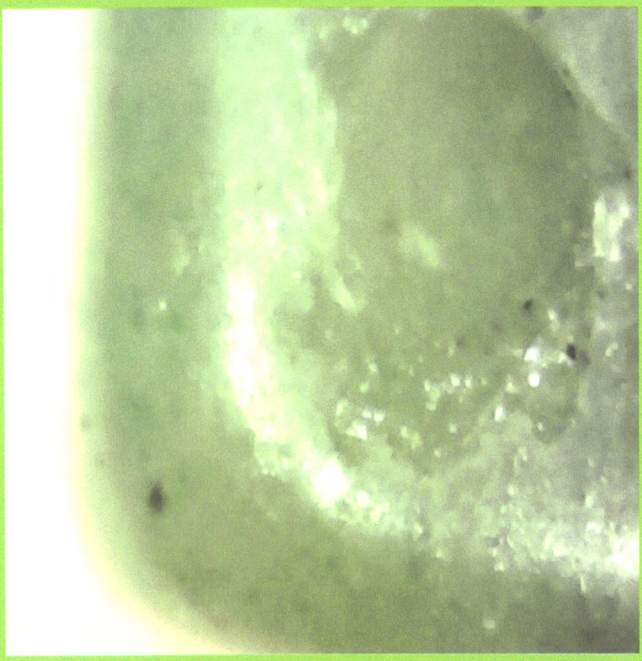
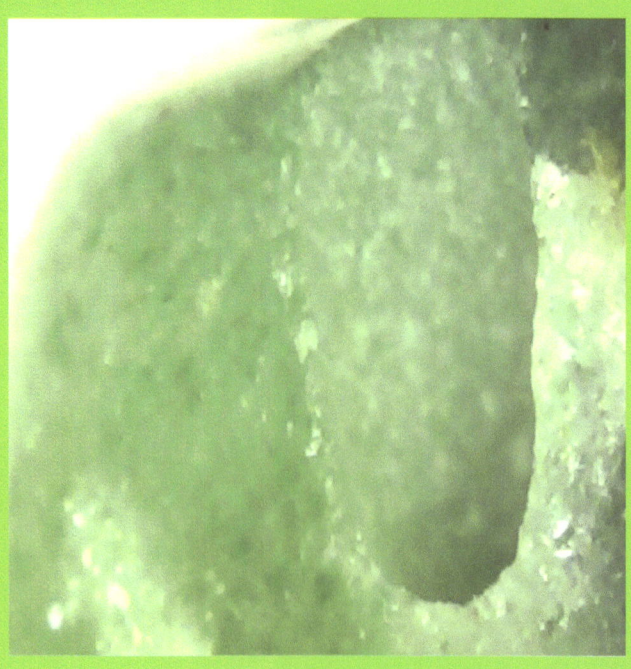

This is ROSE QUARTZ. Isn't that a beautiful name for a pink stone? This is my sister Melody's favorite. She says it makes her feel calm when she looks in this stone. It reminds me of water with the wind blowing over it. It is one of the most interesting stones. I see jewelry made of this in the store all the time. I wonder if this is what is in my mom's box? Maybe a necklace is in the box!

Look how beautiful it is underneath the power of the microscope. Do you think it looks like water? I always think it does. Rose Quartz is similar to a little pink crystal. Grandmother explained to me that Rose is her favorite, because that is her name.

She always tells Melody and I, that this is the most beautiful stone of all. She has a smile when she talks of it. Grandmother believes that it makes us peaceful and joyful when we wear things made with this stone. My mother said, "It can calm the heart."

Rose does look like it has moving water. Rose also shimmers with color inside. I can't see that shimmer of colors like the rainbow until I put it underneath the microscope. Look at the picture on the left. At the top of the picture there is a pointed looking peak that is glowing like a rainbow of color. It has purple in it. Did I tell you purple was my favorite?

I am going to show you one more before I go to sleep. I am tired, but this stone is so wonderful under the microscope, I just have to show you. It is called MOONSTONE. Grandfather has a lot of this. He has some that appear to have little rainbows running through it. Some are pinkish and some are golden. This one is a golden and white mix. It looks like the colors of the moon in the light, and it seems as if little rivers run through it. Amazing!!!!!

Moonstone. Isn't it beautiful? Tomorrow I will show you a group of all of the stones together under the microscope. It will be a beautiful picture under the microscope of how they all look together at once. Good night. I will be dreaming about the treasure box. Just one more day until I turn TEN!

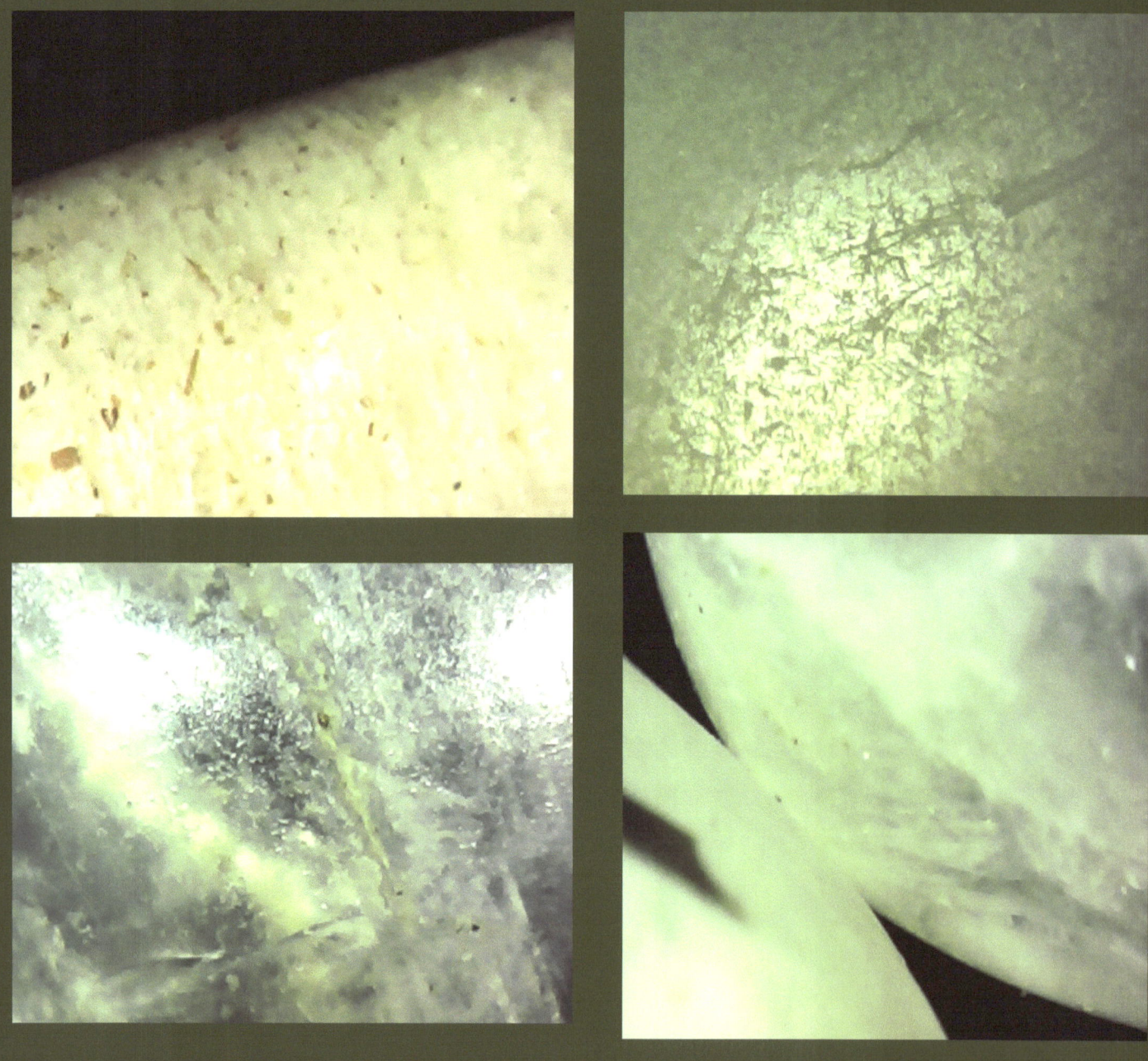

GOOD MORNING. I AM SO EXCITED. TOMORROW IS MY
10TH BIRTHDAY!
HERE ARE THE STONES TOGETHER. LET'S LOOK AT THEM
ALL AT ONCE in a group, then under the microscope as a
group.

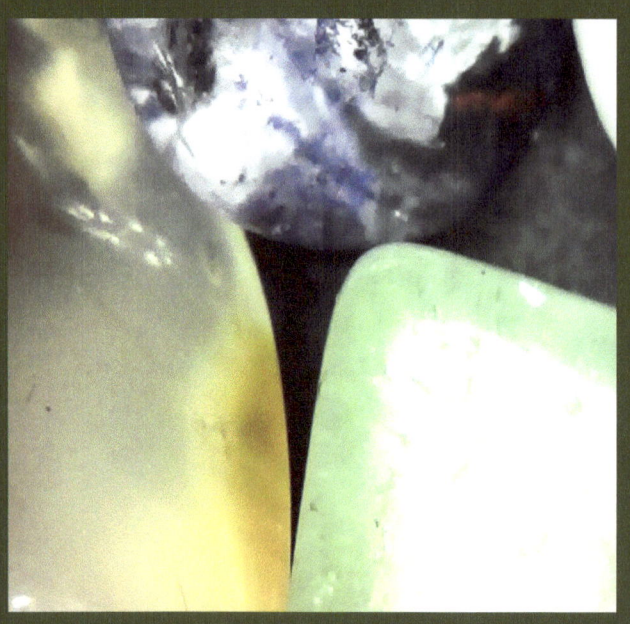 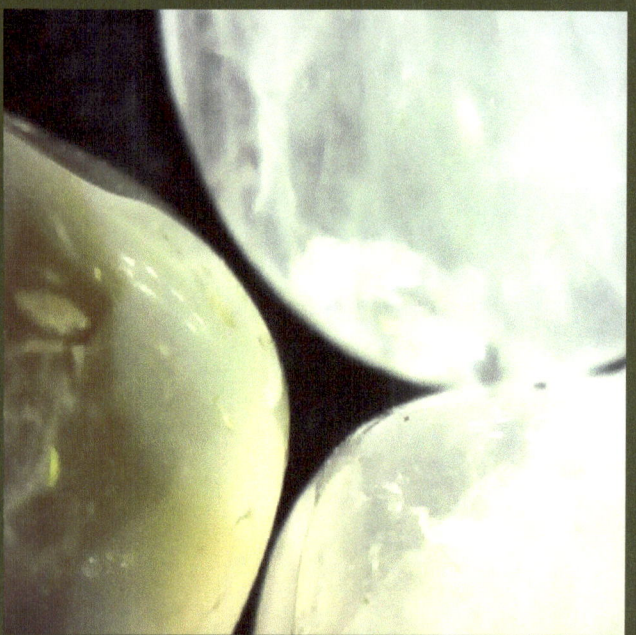

Here they all are. The first picture is an Amethyst, an Aventurine and a Carnelian.
The second picture is a Moonstone, Citrine and a Rose Quartz.
I dreamed last night that all of the stones were singing happy birthday to me. They were even shaking around and dancing together. When I tried to pick one up, all of them ran together and jumped up on my mothers treasure box. I guess I was really thinking a lot about the treasure box before I went to sleep. One more day. I know my birthday will be special even if the treasure box is not my gift.
When I turn TEN, I will feel much older because I will have two numbers in my age instead of one.
Grandfather told me to get ready for a very special day! He must know a very good secret about my birthday. Maybe he has another little stone to add to my collection.

I am so excited. It is still early and I just want to go to bed and wake up turning 10-years-old. I am trying so hard to be patient. Tomorrow can't come fast enough.

I decided that even if I don't get this box, that will be fine. I will tell my mother that I just must know what is inside. I just have to know even if it isn't time for me to have the box.

I asked my Grandfather about it, but, he only told me that one day I would be certain to know, and it would be a beautiful thing to see and find out about. He would not tell me anything else. Father would not either. No one seems to have a clue what is inside except mother, or if they do, they are not sharing it with me.

I will learn to have patience by waiting, OR, I could sneak in there and find out for myself. I keep talking to myself about it. Wouldn't you want to know? Turning 10 is so important. There are two numbers in your age when you turn 10. Something big should happen! Something important! It's early, but I am going to bed and let the morning come. Ten---Here I come!

I opened my eyes this morning to find the most beautiful box sitting upon my night stand. It was THE BOX!   I did not hear anyone come into my room. Mother must have quietly brought this surprise to me. Oh, it is more beautiful than ever. And, look, two of my favorite stones sitting on top for my collection. I wonder if I am supposed to touch it? I wonder if I am supposed to open it up and look inside? Oh my, I am TEN.

I am about to find out something very important. I have so many questions in my head and I haven't even looked inside. What am I supposed to do with it once I know? What about when it is time to give it to someone else? What about—oh, I must find Mother. I'm so nervous. "HAPPY 10TH BIRTHDAY TO ME!"

"HAPPY BIRTHDAY MY SWEET DAUGHTER, MELANIE," mother said.   She WHISPERED to me, "Open it, look inside."   My hands are shaking and the box has the most beautiful carvings on it. The detail is white and pearly. A treasure box like this just has to have a marvelous secret inside. The time has come for me to find out what it is. I will open it very slowly. I can see that it is old and the little clasp in the back is broken on one side, but it is still so special to know it is mine.

Now I will gently open the lid and find out the Secret! I will count to TEN and then lift the top!
1-2-3-4-5-6-7-8-9----10!!!!!!!!!!

HOW BEAUTIFUL! It Is a Crystal. I don't have
a crystal like this. It has so many lights inside,
I can see them. It has a wound on the end.
Oh, I must take it out and look at it closer.
Let me lay it out on the table in the light.

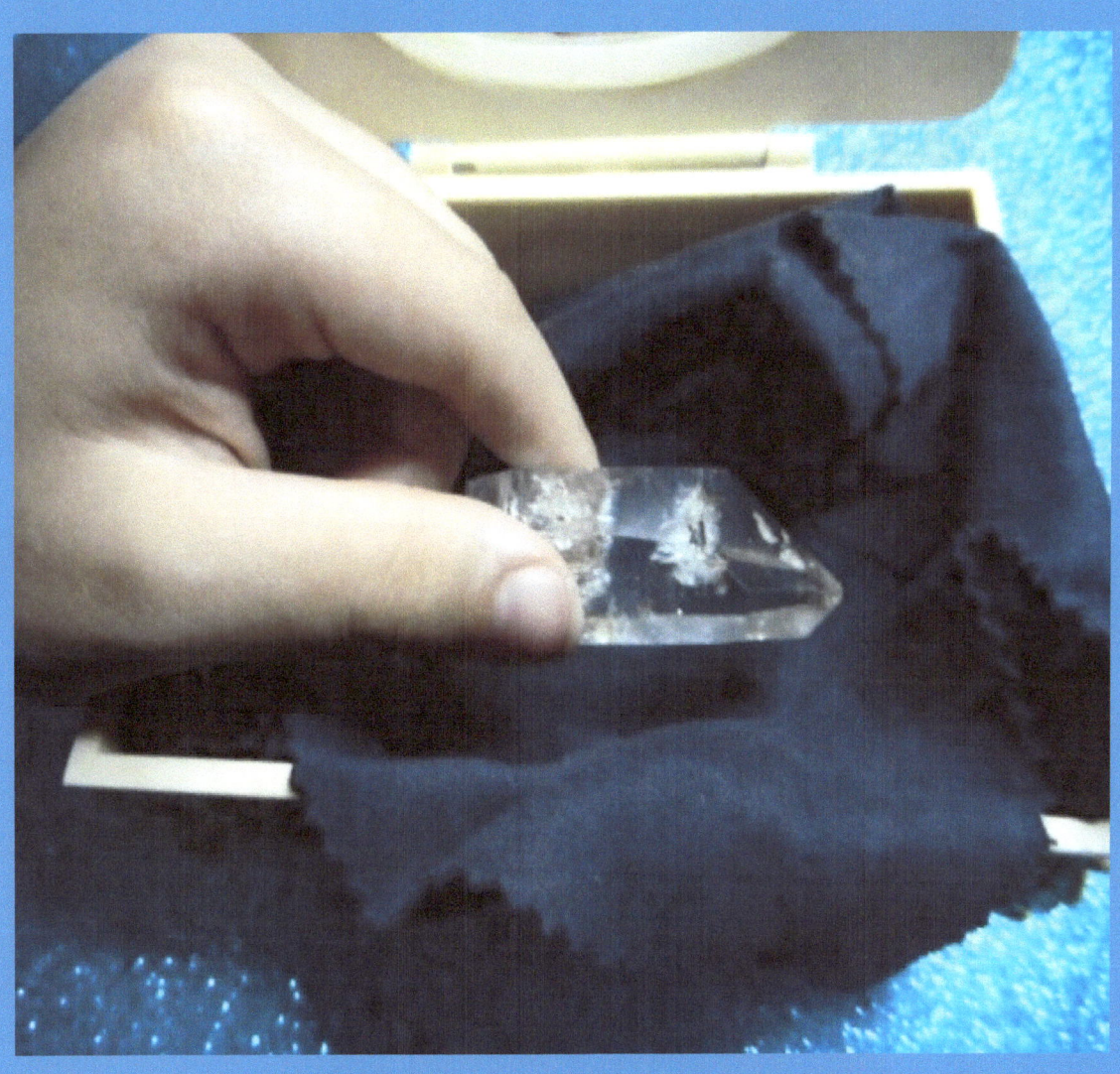

The crystal has an end that looks like it was broken. It also looks like it healed itself from a very long time ago. I can see so many little things inside. I SEE LINES INSIDE! This is an important Crystal. Grandfather told me these have SECRETS inside. I am taking this straight to my microscope and find out what the secrets are. I want Mother to see inside with me. I bet she has never seen inside of it the way I can. This will be our present to each other. We will find THE SECRET OF THE BROKEN STONE!

The lines look just like a triangle. A window inside. It looks like it has mountains and water with clouds at the top. This is the most special stone I have ever seen. I can't believe it is mine. But I know there is so much more to see within the length. The lines must have been made by something or someone. They are perfect. They are perfect deep carved lines, just like a triangle.

"Look Mother, it is so beautiful." "Yes it is, Melanie," said Mother.

"Windows into another world, that is what it looks like to me," said Mother. It looks like you could dive off of a cliff into a pool of water.

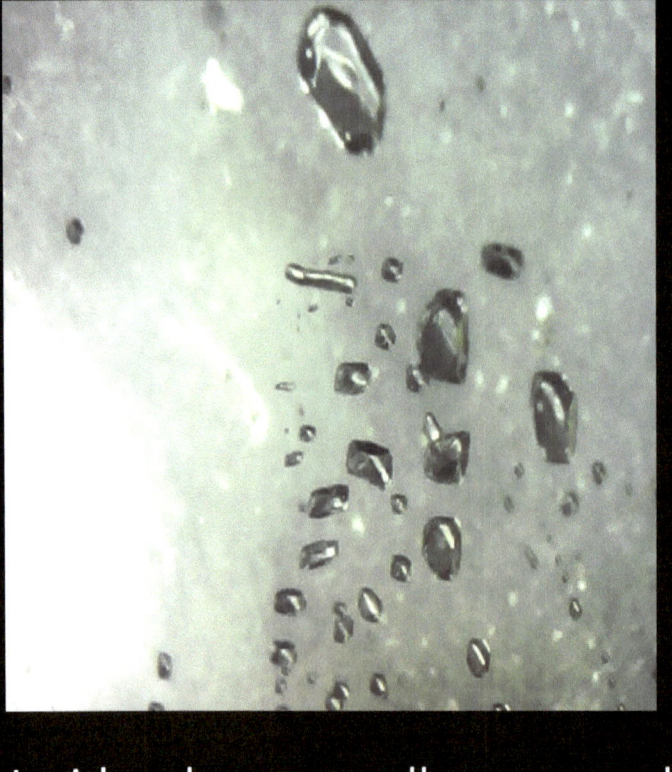
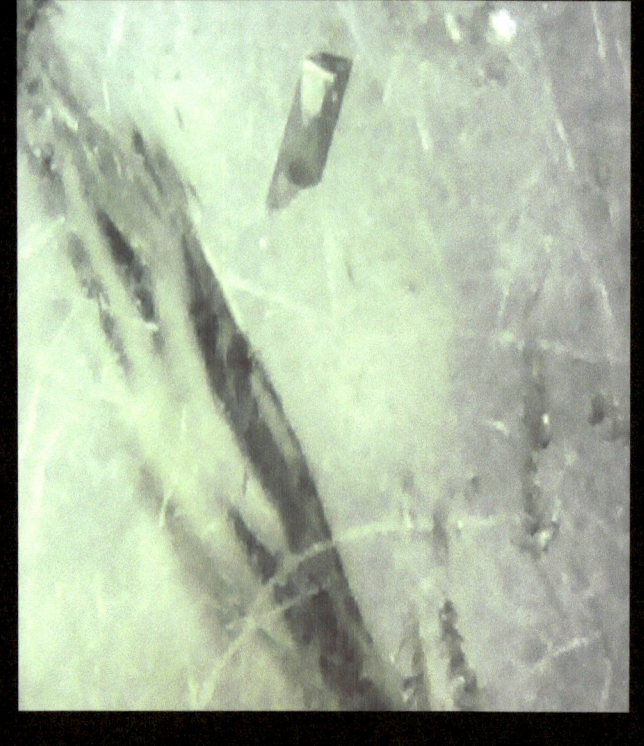

Inside, along a small area were bubbles, just like water droplets. This must be the oldest water in the entire world. Sharp little crystals seem to be growing within the walls. Oh, how I want to know where it came from, who found it, and why it has been such a beautiful Secret passed down. I must know more.

Every time I move the scope there is a new spot to find with a new secret. It is so beautiful. It is very hard, cold, and looks as if ice has formed on it.
The water in the large bubble has slight movement. Grandfather said these were called "Enhydro Crystal Quartz." That means crystals with tiny water drops inside.

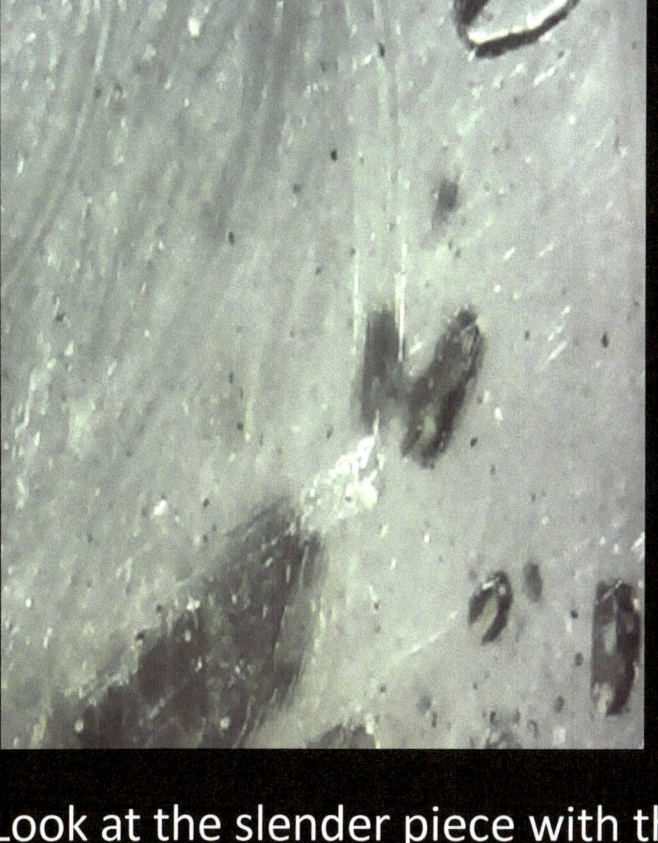
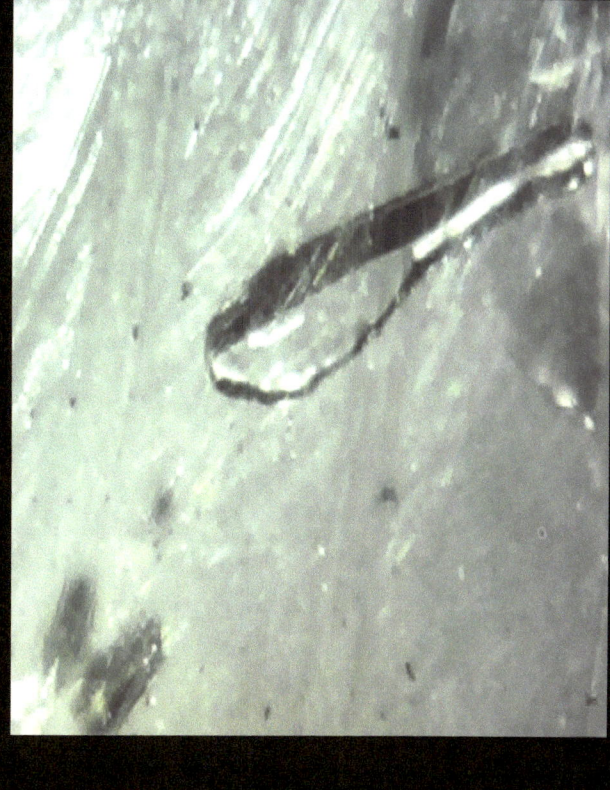

Look at the slender piece with the tail on it. It appears as if something is swimming in the center, but it isn't moving. I think it reminds me of a Stingray fish.

As I sat with my mother looking at the most precious stone I had ever seen, she began to almost whisper to me the story of why it is here, why it is passed down, and why on the 10th birthday it becomes a gift of legacy to the eldest girl child.

As I listened closely I felt taken far back in time to a place where caves were quiet and dark, the earth holding tight to her secrets.

Mother began her story by telling me it belonged to my Great-Great Grandfather. He obtained the stone when he was ten-years-old, just like me, but in a very different way.

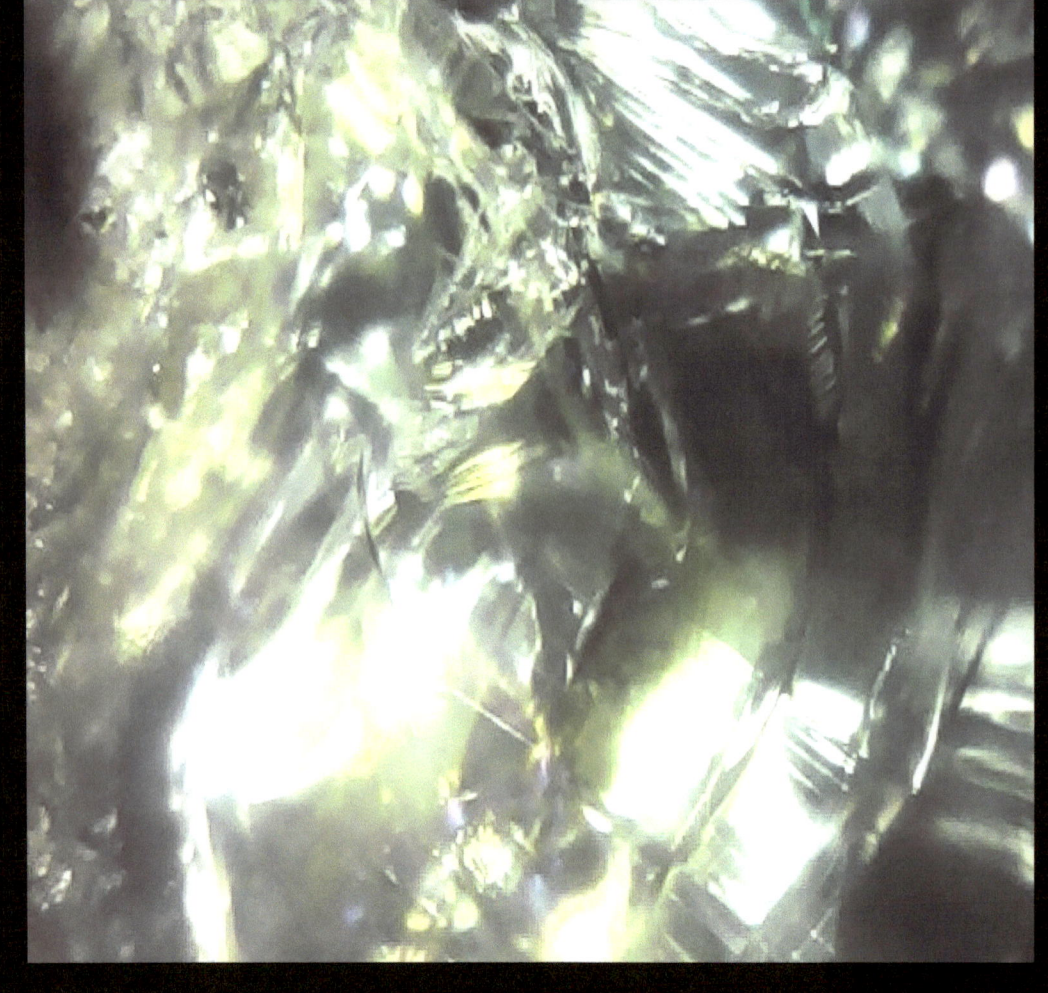

My Great-Great Grandfather had gone to work with his
father one morning. His father mined for coal. He couldn't
help much because he was to young to lift the heavy buckets
of coal, so he began to walk around and investigate what
was around the area. Suddenly, his eyes caught a glimpse of
rainbow flashes coming from across the mining area, so he
drew closer. There was a cave, a cave no one had found
before. The entrance was nearly completely closed but
there was a small slit near the entrance. The sun was
shining right into that crevice and Great-Great Grandfather
could see rainbow lights flickering.

Amazed by the lights, he ran toward the cave to see what it was. There in the crevice of the tight opening to the cave was a crystal, stuck in the center. The sun beamed upon it causing it to flash all the colors of the rainbow. As he worked to free the stone, he could tell it had been hurt. One end of the crystal looked as if water had flowed over and over it to help it heal. Great-Great Grandfather couldn't free the stone easily, but with time and very careful tugging, he succeeded, releasing it from its tight home. In his hand laid the most beautiful crystal he had ever seen. There had never been one found here before.

Running swiftly back to tell his father what he had found, as he turned away from the cave, he heard a loud crashing sound and thousands of rainbow flashes appeared.

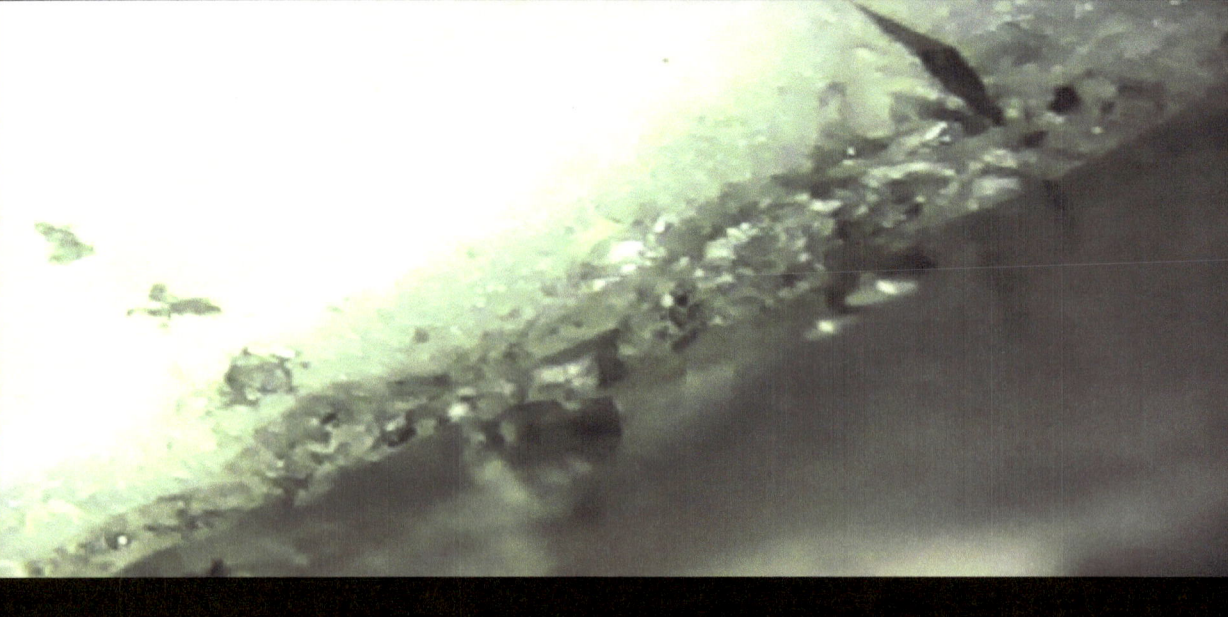

His small crystal must have been holding everything together just like a key. When he released the crystal, the entire cavern awakened. The rocks that had held the entrance closed since the beginning of time had now broken open to reveal crystals as old as the Earth, standing as tall as the trees. The light coming from them glowed like ice at the North Pole. Rainbows flashed, and the sound of dripping water could be heard. Great-Great Grandfather ran as fast as he could , calling for his father as he fled.

"Father, Father," he yelled. His father, which would be my Great-Great-Great Grandfather, by the way, came quickly towards him, thinking he was hurt. When he reached him, his attention was quickly amazed at the site not far in front of them. The cavern laid open, revealing The Secret of the Broken Stone.

They walked closer and closer until they reached the opening, stopping at the entrance, viewing the breathtaking wonders flickering before them. As my Great-Great Grandfather explained the keystone, and how he saw it, his father told him to always protect it. "Never reveal the location of the doorway," he told him. Energy seemed to blast forth from the cave.

As time went by, and he grew up, he married my Great-Great Grandmother. He bought a small white treasure box, and placed the stone inside, giving it to her as a wedding present with the secret it held; *the location of the crystal cave.*

As my mother and I sat looking deep inside through the microscope, we smiled because only she and I and grandmother knew of the treasure.

Whispering to me, mother said, "Give it to your daughter when she is ten."

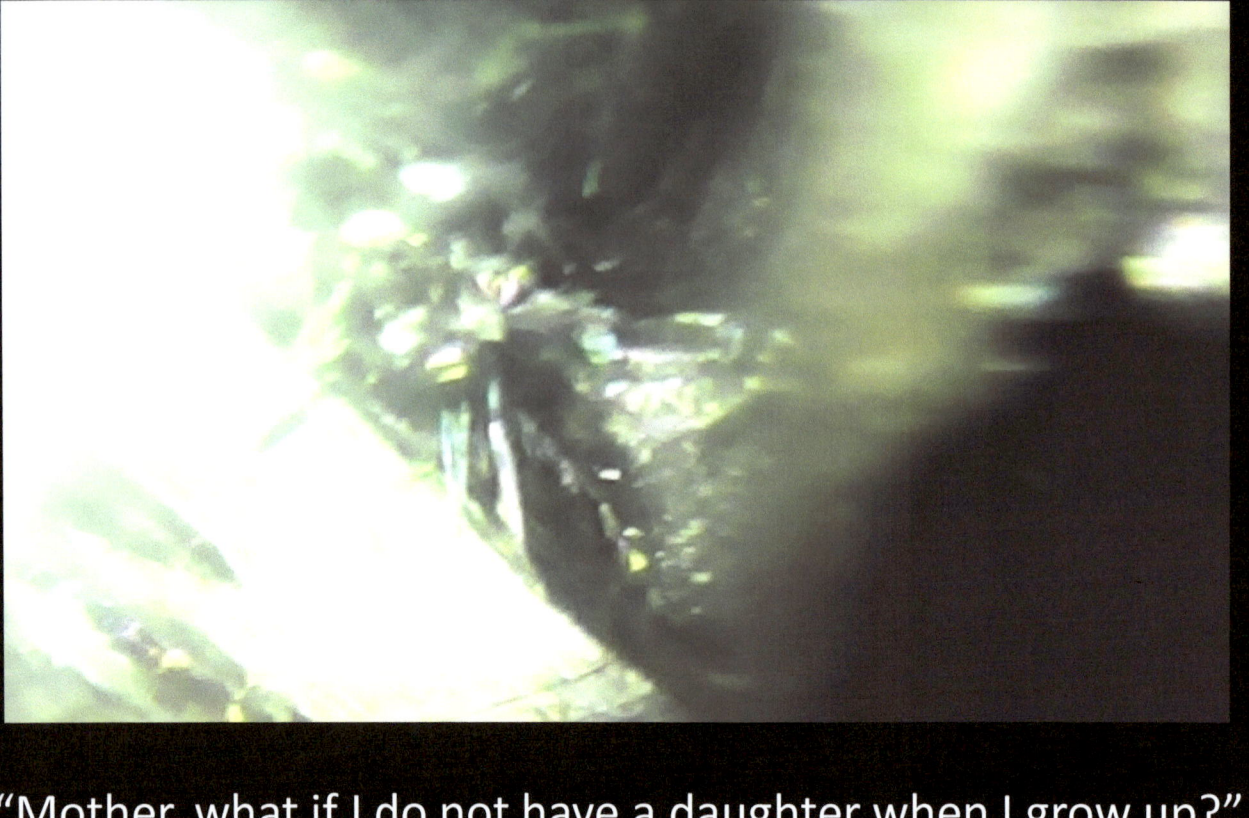

"Mother, what if I do not have a daughter when I grow up?"
"Then you shall give it to your son," mother said. "Mother,
what if I have no son, or a daughter to pass The Secret of the
Broken Stone to?" As I looked at my mother and she looked
at me, a whisper came from behind our chair. It was
Grandmother.
She said, "It has never been a decision one has had to make
since the gift was found by your Great-Great Grandfather,
but should it happen in your life, you shall take the stone to
the Secret location and place it at the entrance. There, it will
wait until the sun decides who shall find *The Secret of the
Broken Stone*, the same way it found your Great-Great
Grandfather. A new family will be starting a new treasure
secret for their lives with a wonderful journey through time."

As I turned the microscope off, I picked up the stone, placing it back into the tiny treasure box from which it came, and knew that I would take it out many times again.

There were faces, and lights , pathways and windows, even a pyramid inside.   The more I searched, the more I found the Secrets within. All the magic of the beginning of time was waiting for me to investigate under the microscope.

I knew one day, I would have to part with it. Only time would tell me which decision would be made. Would it be passed to my child, or back to the cavern as the key it was before? The Secret of the Broken Stone belongs to me now. I am ten, and one day there may be a very special birthday for someone else. Mine has been beautiful.

WHAT DO YOU REMEMBER FROM THE STORY?

What is the name of the girl who was turning ten?

What is her sister's name?

Can you name three things that were shown to you while Melanie was passing time with you before her birthday arrived?

What stone do you like the most under the microscope?

What type of crystal is The Broken Stone called?

What did her Great-Great Grandfather's father do at work?

How was the stone found?

What happened to the cave entrance when the keystone crystal was removed?

What was her Great-Great Grandfather told not to do?

How tall were the crystals inside the cavern cave?

What did he place the stone in to protect it?

How old was he when he found it?

How old was Melanie when she received it?

What person did her Great-Great Grandfather give the stone to, and why?

What is Melanie to do if she has no one to pass the stone to one day?

What things were seen in the stone under the microscope?

What stone is Melanie's favorite, and what color is it?

Where did Melanie's mother keep the stone?

Would you be able to keep The Secret of the Broken Stone, and tell no one of the location of the cave?

THE SECRET OF THE BROKEN STONE –BOOK 2
MICROSCOPIC WORLD SERIES

THE MOSS—BOOK 1
MICROSCOPIC WORLD SERIES

COLLECT THEM ALL

Visit my author page to find out more about me.
WWW.AMAZON.COM/AUTHOR/BJMORRISON

WEBSITE: WWW.THEHEARTBEATOFWORDS.COM

BLOG: WWW.THEHEARTBEATOFWORDS.BLOGSPOT.COM

Book 3 in the series will be shortly revealed.
The title is: The House in the Trees

LOOK FOR MY UPCOMING NOVELS IN 2016